J. H. Caldwell, J. E. Bryant

The Georgia Question

Before the Judiciary Committee of the United States Senate

J. H. Caldwell, J. E. Bryant

The Georgia Question
Before the Judiciary Committee of the United States Senate

ISBN/EAN: 9783337161514

Printed in Europe, USA, Canada, Australia, Japan

Cover: Foto ©Suzi / pixelio.de

More available books at **www.hansebooks.com**

THE GEORGIA QUESTION

BEFORE THE

Judiciary Committee of the United States Senate

ARGUMENTS

OF

HON. J. H. CALDWELL

AND

HON. J. E. BRYANT.

The delegation was composed of the following gentlemen :

Hon. J. E. BRYANT,
Hon. J. H. CALDWELL, } *Members of the Legislature.*
Hon. C. K. OSGOOD,
Hon. A. J. WILLIAMS, }
Hon. N. L. ANGIER, *State Treasurer.*
Col. JOHN BOWLES.

WASHINGTON, D. C.
GIBSON BROTHERS, PRINTERS
1870.

Mr. CALDWELL, addressing the committee in behalf of the delegation, said :

Mr. Chairman and Gentlemen of the Judiciary Committee: We are Georgians, and as such come to represent our State in one of the most critical emergencies that has ever fallen to the lot of any State in this great Republic. Although we are all Republicans, and could, were it necessary, recount toils, sacrifices, and perils attending our efforts to establish a Republican party in our State ; yet, for the time being, we cease to be mere partisans, and appeal to you as Georgians, concerned for the well-being of our State and the future peace and prosperity of our people. We propose, therefore, in the name and behalf of those whom, as a delegation, we represent, to present a plain, unvarnished statement of facts, with the inferences which they convey, trusting to your wisdom to devise a remedy for existing evils, and to your sense of justice to redress the wrongs of which we complain.

Georgia, as you are aware, proceeded to carry out in good faith the reconstruction acts of the 39th Congress. A convention framed a constitution, which was submitted to the people for their ratification. It was ratified by a large majority ; the great mass of the voters, some two hundred thousand in number, participating in the election. It was as free and impartial as any election that was ever held in Georgia, the polls being protected generally under the military supervision of Major General Meade, the district commander. At the same time a Governor, county officers, members of Congress, forty-four State senators, and one hundred and seventy-three representatives were elected ; two counties, entitled to one member each, making no returns. The constitution being submitted to Congress, was, in the main, approved by that body, and an act was passed declaring the State of Georgia entitled to representation in Congress whenever the legislature should adopt certain fundamental conditions.

On the 25th June, 1868, General Meade issued a proclamation convening the members elect at Atlanta, on the 4th July following. The names of those who were declared elected by General Meade appear in that proclamation, and it is printed in the journal of the House of Representatives for 1868, which we herewith present for your inspection. The members were sworn in by Judge Erskine, in the presence of General Meade and Rufus B. Bullock, Governor elect, who was acting at the time as Provisional Governor. Each member was sworn to support the Constitution of the United States and of the State of Georgia. No other oath was required. The omission of any other was in consequence of the advice of certain members of the Reconstruction Committee, and approved by General Grant. From that time each member was bound, in all the subsequent legislation in which he participated, by his oath to support the constitution of the State, and we are not aware that Congress has passed any act since then that released him from the obligation of that oath. No question was raised, either at the time the members were qualified or before, as to the eligibility of any of them on any ground whatever, but all who were named in the proclamation were allowed to qualify. Each house proceeded to elect and qualify its officers. The president and all the other officers of the senate were regular nominees of the Republican party. The house elected the Republican nominee for speaker, and then adjourned until Monday, the 6th July. The members split up and divided on the other officers, the Democrats electing the clerk and messenger, and the Republicans the door-keeper. On a joint ballot, as afterwards appeared, the Republicans had a clear majority of thirteen.

As soon as the two houses were organized, Provisional Governor Bullock suggested to General Meade that there

were persons holding seats in each house who were ineligible under the fourteenth article, and the General
ordered both houses to suspend all other business and proceed to inquire into the eligibility of the members. A
resolution was adopted by each house, after the investigation,
declaring all the members eligible. This was done when
there was a clear Republican majority in each branch, else
neither could have elected its Republican nominees. The
result was not due, therefore, as has been charged, to a disloyal temper on the part of a majority of either house. In
all elections in either house, or both conjointly, the members
were called *eo nomine*, by the proper officer, and they
voted *viva voce*, as the constitution requires. General
Meade approved the course of each house in the investigation and determining of the question of eligibility, and the
legislature immediately ratified the fourteenth article, and
adopted the fundamental conditions required by Congress.
Hon. Rufus B. Bullock was then inaugurated as the permanent Governor, *he swearing to support the Constitution of the
United States and of the State of Georgia.* His term of office,
according to an ordinance of the convention, providing for
the first election under the new constitution, was to extend
from the time of his inauguration till four years from the
following January, or until January, 1873, when his suc-
cessor, to be elected in November preceding, should be
qualified. One-half of the senators were to hold till January, 1873, when their successors should be qualified, and
the other half, with all the representatives, until January,
1871.

The theory of his Excellency now is, that the late act of
Congress for promoting reconstruction in Georgia invali-
dates all acts of the legislature which preceded it, and that
consequently his own term of office is extended till four years
from next January; the term of one-half of the senators is
extended for the same period, and the terms of the other
half, and of all the representatives, till January, 1873, thus
giving to all an extension of two years beyond the time meant

by the constitutional convention or intended by their constit-
uencies. Such is the pretension based upon the plain and
simple act passed by Congress in December last. But it
will be well to show how inconsistent such a presumption is
with former declarations and acts of his Excellency.

In his inaugural address, he congratulated the country on
the *completion of reconstruction in Georgia!* The same day
he gave a banquet, rejoicing with his friends over the restoration of the State to her place in the Union. But, mark
you, this was before the election of United States Senators.

*In due time that election was held, and the result was
different from what his Excellency anticipated. Hon.
Joshua Hill, a distinguished Union man, and a Republican,
was elected for the long term. Hon. H. V. M. Miller, an old
Whig, a member of the Constitutional Convention, an
earnest friend of reconstruction, chairman of the committee
appointed to revise the work of the eight committees to whom
was assigned the different parts of the constitution, advocat-
ing before the people the ratification of the new constitution,
was elected to the short term. This was done without any
concert or agreement between them, Mr. Hill's supporters
on the first ballot being only Union men and Republicans.
Leaving off all those who voted for Mr. Miller, who have
since been declared ineligible, he had a clear majority of
three. By the same rule, Hon. Joseph E. Brown, the
regular Republican nominee, got a majority of one. (See
Appendix.)

Governor Bullock certified officially to the election of
Messrs. Hill and Miller, and in his certificate declared that
they were legally elected.

After the election of senators the legislature went into an
election for State house officers, and all the Republican
nominees were elected—still showing that the composition of
the legislature was decidedly Republican. If all who, since
their election, have been declared ineligible, are counted
off, as in the estimate made for the Senators, it will be seen
that they were all elected by a majority of the voters. Thus

the Governor's favorite plea for a re-election of State house officers, viz: that there were ineligible members in both houses who voted in those elections, cannot avail him for setting their election aside, for they were elected in spite of the ineligible members, not one of whom voted for them. For proof of this, I refer you to the journals of the two houses. In various ways, but especially in all his public official acts and signatures, Governor Bullock did recognize or assume the validity of the first organization of the General Assembly. General Meade did the same; Congress did the same; at any rate the House of Representatives, in the very act by which certain Representatives from Georgia were seated.

This statement of facts thus far covers about two months— we think about sixty-five days from the first meeting of the General Assembly on the 4th July, 1868. During this time elections were held, and many acts were passed by the legislature, some of them involving grave financial interests, and yet no one ever suggested the idea, nor did any one dream that the idea ever would be suggested, that the legislature was illegally organized, or that any act had been done that in the slightest degree vitiated its proceedings.

Then, in the month of September, came the expulsion of the colored members. That act we have ever regarded as unconstitutional and unjust, and do not defend or excuse it. But we would respectfully ask you to consider the dangerous use which has been made of it by the Governor and those who are acting in concert with him. He has evidently made it the grand salient point from which to reach results which he would gladly have had some excuse to secure without it. He has made it the occasion to ask Congress to pass a law giving into his hands the most extraordinary powers, powers which he has seen fit to assume, although the act passed by Congress does not grant them. The colored members were expelled partly by Republican votes, and that under the rul av of a speaker of the house of representatives who was It is nor Bullock's favorite candidate in the recent election for speaker. Some Republicans voted with the Democrats for their expulsion, and others refused to vote at all. Some of those who voted for their expulsion, and a number of those who refused to vote at all, are now with his Excellency asking that all former proceedings of the legislature be set aside as invalid; while with us there are some who defended the colored members in the house, and voted against their expulsion, and we beseech you to see that the act of Congress is carried out strictly, in good faith, without any perversion of its meaning or violation of its provisions. The Governor has made the expulsion of the colored members the occasion for the accomplishment of purposes which lie deeper than was anticipated by Congress when they passed the act of December last. It has long been manifest to some true men of the Republican party in Georgia, that a restoration of the colored members and the purging of the legislature were only ostensible, or, at best, but subordinate objects. Some ground has been eagerly sought after on which he might not only secure a reorganization of the legislature, but the ripping up of every act preceding that reorganization, and he assumes that he has authority under the recent act of Congress to accomplish that object, and he comes here to ask that you tolerate his assumption. He has proceeded without a single check in the execution of his purpose, and he wishes still to pursue his object without restraint. His assumption is this: that the late act of Congress makes the whole State government, as constituted under the administration of General Meade, a nullity; that there has been no meeting of the legislature elected in April, 1868, except the one which he was authorized by the late act to convene; that this is its first session; that there has been no legal election of United States Senators or State house officers, and, that, per consequence, all the official terms must be extended two years beyond what was intended at the time of the election. Such is his theory of the present status of our civil government. Other consequences must follow as the practical effect of this theory. There are three justices of the supreme court, seventeen judges of the superior court, and the same number of solicitors general, all of whom are nominated by the Governor. Besides these, there is a large number of notaries public, who are *ex-officio* justices of the peace, appointed by the Governor. All these must be removed and their places filled by reappointments. Thus, his theory sweeps down our entire judiciary as at present organized. But this is not the worst. We have eminent jurists, whose reputation for ability is co-extensive with our country. Some of these, and other high officials, have become personally objectionable to his Excellency, and he wishes you to let him displace them by the practical operation of his theory. He would have their places vacated under the operation of your act, that he may fill them with his new favorites.

Sad as are these consequences of the Governor's assumption, there are others which are most pernicious to a body of legislators. A personal friend of his Excellency, a leading member of the Senate, on the first day of the present session, the 10th of January, was explaining to me what the effect of the Governor's theory would be, including all the points I have mentioned ; and emphasizing that which relates to an extension of the official terms, especially of membership in the legislature, he added, with an air of triumph : *"And you know that the members will not vote themselves out of the legislature when they have the chance to remain in for two years longer."* I give the substance of the remark, but I have seen with what effect the idea was circulated among the members, and I know that his Excellency is too skilful a politician not to take advantage of such an inducement to gain adherents to his theory. But what must the country think, and what must be the effect upon the Republican party throughout the nation, if Congress should lend its sanction to an extension of the terms of office in a State under such circumstances? We trust that, in the wisdom of your honorable committee, measures may be taken which will avert the calamity that we fear would ensue.

It is inconceivable that honorable Senators and Representatives could ever have meant that their act should serve the double purpose to which the Governor has turned it. It is inconceivable that they would lend the influence of their great names to a plain measure to do only certain things, and at the same time have a covert design that it should be used to accomplish other things besides those expressly enjoined ; in short, to require nothing more than to reseat the expelled members, purge the legislature of ineligible members, and ratify the fifteenth article, and at the same time purpose that the Governor should use it to overturn the government that had been previously established. The Governor had no authority from the act of Congress to call upon any one to expound the oath contained in it, nor to appoint a clerk *pro tem.* to organize the house, nor to claim that he is merely a provisional governor, nor to treat the legislature as a provisional legislature, nor to prevent any one from taking one of the prescribed oaths, nor to invoke the aid of the military in investigating the eligibility of members, nor to put out of the legislature any one who might be declared ineligible by a body unknown to the law, nor to put others in the places of those who were thus declared ineligible, nor to require the re-ratification of the fourteenth amendment, or re-adoption of the fundamental conditions required by the 40th Congress. Yet, assuming that he had all these powers conferred upon him by that act, he has been guilty of the following flagrant violations of the law :

1. In calling upon Attorney General Farrow to give a written opinion of the scope of the oath required by Congress.

2. In endeavoring, by the operation of that opinion, which was published in the Atlanta papers the day before the legislature convened, to deter some members from taking the oath who were not excluded by the fourteenth amendment. This was done under a mere semblance of authority, for in reality it had no more than the opinion of any private individual ; but the approval of General Terry caused it to assume

a gravity which would not otherwise be attributed to it. Why should this unauthorized opinion be so extensively promulgated, when that of Attorney General Hoar, which has authority, has been withheld?

3. By the appointment of A. L. Harris, one of his Excellency's employees on the State road, as clerk *pro tem.*, to organize the house. As each member was sworn to support the State constitution, and the Code was adopted by that constitution as the law of the State, and the act failing to point out an officer who should organize the house, the Code, in sections 169 and 170, shows how it should be organized. .

4. By appointing a registrar in bankruptcy to swear in the members. The Code requires that it should be done by a judge of the supreme or superior courts.

5. By ordering the arbitrary ruling of the clerk *pro tem.*, who refused to entertain a motion from any member, even on questions pertaining to the organization; who adjourned the house whenever he pleased, from time to time, without a motion from any member; and who showed, throughout, a determination to have an organization which should be, as far as possible, subservient to the schemes of the Governor.

6. Asking for a military commission to investigate the eligibility of members.

7. By preventing a number of persons in both houses from qualifying, who, according to the decision of the board in other cases, would have been declared eligible.

8. By delaying the organization of the house, and harassing members who were afterwards declared eligible, causing them to appear before a board of officers not provided for by law, to sit in judgment upon their eligibility.

9. By causing some who had qualified to be prohibited from taking part in the organization of their respective houses.

10. By causing two persons, Mr. Wilcher and Mr. Bennett, who were declared eligible, from participating in the organization of the house.

11. By invoking the aid of the military under pretence of enforcing and executing the provisions of the act, no resistance being offered to the organization of either house under the act. On the contrary, all the members showed a willingness to organize in strict conformity to its provisions, and the only opposition which was manifested was to the illegal manner of the proceedings.

12. The manner in which his Excellency suffered persons to be intimidated and prevented from qualifying is illustrated in the case of some who were threatened, so that they became apprehensive of being harassed by prosecutions if they should take the oath. Inducements were held out to some of them, which caused them unwarily to commit themselves to positions which seemed to imply a confession of ineligibility. They were advised to make application to Congress for a relief from disabilities, when, in fact, when their cases were properly understood, they had none. Promises were held out that in a short time Congress would relieve them, and they could then take their seats. They were not aware of the deception by which they were tricked out of their rights until General Terry's order, No. 9, declared that such applications for relief were confessions of ineligibility.

13. By allowing a senator who had taken the oath to withdraw the same from the office of the secretary of State, thus removing a document that might be needed as evidence in case of a prosecution for perjury.

14. By admitting a number of persons in both houses to seats who had not been elected by popular majorities. The only shadow of law for such a proceeding is in the 121st section of the Code. This section does not refer to members of the legislature at all, for the following reasons:

1. The officers referred to in this section are executive officers, intrusted with the execution of the laws—they are not legislators, charged with the making of laws. The Code is divided into different "Parts;" each "Part" into "Titles;" each "Title" into "Chapters," "Articles," and "Sections."

Sections sometimes have several subdivisions, as the 120th the one immediately preceding the one in question, and closely connected with it. This section is in " Title" three, headed "Executive Department;" Title four is the "Legislative Department," and contains no such provision.

2. The officers alluded to are such as a plurality of votes may elect, but there is no law in Georgia which declares that a plurality may elect a member of the legislature. I challenge the learned judges, who are, with the Governor, here to-day, to point you to the section in our Code that says a plurality can elect a member to the legislature.

3. The officer whose place may be filled by the person having the next highest number of votes must be one who is ineligible under the rules laid down in section 120. Seven classes of persons are there declared to be ineligible to office, and the 14th Article is not enumerated among them.

4. It is unconstitutional to apply this section to a member of the legislature, for the constitution gives to each house the sole right to decide upon the qualifications of its members, and neither the Code nor any legislative enactment can deprive either house of that right.

5. The officers referred to are such as are " commissioned ;" but members of the legislature are not commissioned.

6. There is no precedent in the history of parliamentary proceedings to warrant such action.

15. Others who did not belong to the Governor's party, who were in precisely the same circumstances, presented themselves, and when a motion was made to swear them in, the speaker ruled it out of order, saying that he had received no orders to do so.

Finally, Mr. Chairman and gentlemen of the committee, we beseech you, in behalf of more than a million of our fellow-citizens, to save Georgia from the consequences of so many flagrant violations of the law. We entreat you that the Executive of our State may not be permitted, under a pretence of enforcing law, to override and disregard the plain provisions of the law of Congress. We ask that the wrongs

inflicted by the Governor may be redressed. We beseech
you not to suffer the financial interests of a great but un-
fortunate State to be placed so completely at the mercy of
one who has shown such a reckless disregard of law. We
pray you to rescue our State from a ruin and degradation
that has scarcely been equalled in Poland or Ireland.

APPENDIX.

The following members of the senate were declared ineligible: Anderson, Graham, Moore, Winn, and Collier—5.

The following members of the house were declared ineligible: Burtz, Crawford, Drake, Donaldson, Brinson,* Ellis, of Spalding; George, Goff, Hudson, Johnson, of Wilcox; Kellogg, Meadows, Nunn, Penland, Rouse, Smith, of Coffee; Surreney, Taliaferro, Williams, of Dooly, McCullough, and Long—21.

Bradley, of the senate, had been declared ineligible as a convicted felon, under the constitution of Georgia, before the colored members were expelled.

Upon the election of Senators for the long term—

Mr. Hill received 110 votes.

Mr. Brown received 94 votes.

Mr. Stephens received 1 vote.

Mr. Styles received 1 vote.

Of the persons declared ineligible, Mr. Hill received the votes of the following:

Anderson and Moore in the senate. In the house, he received the votes of Burtz, Crawford, Drake, Donaldson, Ellis, of Spalding; George, Goff, Hudson, Johnson, of Wilcox; Kellogg, Meadows, Nunn, Penland, Rouse, Taliaferro, and Williams, of Dooly, Long,† and McCullough—total, 20. These deducted from his entire vote leave 90 votes of persons admitted to be eligible.

The vote cast for Mr. Styles was by Mr. Graham, who was declared ineligible.

Of persons declared ineligible, Mr. Brown received the votes of Surreney and Bradley.

---

* Collier and Brinson did not vote for Miller.

† Mr. Long was sick at home, but can take the oath. Mr. Thomasson, the person getting the next highest number of votes, has been seated in his place.

The vote of the eligible members would stand thus—
Hill, 90.
Brown, 92.
Stephens, 1.

In the election of senator for the short term, the table in the journal of the house of representatives shows that—

Mr. Miller has 120 votes ; but upon counting the names of the persons recorded as voting, it appears that he received 117 votes.

Mr. Blodgett received 72 votes.

Mr. Seward received 13 votes.

Mr. Akerman received 6 votes.

Of the persons declared ineligible, Mr. Miller received the votes of the following :

Anderson, Graham, Moore, and Winn, of the senate ; Burtz, Crawford, Drake, Donaldson, Ellis, of Spalding ; George, Goff, Hudson, Johnson, of Wilcox ; Kellogg, Meadows, Nunn, Penland, Rouse, Smith, of Coffee ; Surrency, Taliaferro, Williams, of Dooly, Long, and McCullough ; total, 24. These subtracted from his entire vote leave him 93 votes of those admitted to be eligible.

Mr. Blodgett received, of ineligible persons, one vote Bradley, of the senate.

Of persons declared eligible—
Mr. Miller received... 93
Mr. Blodgett...71
Mr. Seward...13
Mr. Akerman...6
                                                                          ——
                                                                          90

Making Mr. Miller a majority, of all who are admitted to be eligible, of three. All this will appear from the journal of the house of representatives herewith submitted to the Judiciary Committee.

HON. J. E. BRYANT,

OF GEORGIA,

Before the Judiciary Committee of the United States Senate.

Mr. BRYANT said :

Mr. Chairman and Gentlemen of the Judiciary Committee:

A citizen of Georgia, a Republican member of the General
Assembly of that State, I appear before you to inform you
that the act of Congress, passed on the 22d day of December
last, to promote the reconstruction of the State of Georgia,
has been violated in the organization of the General Assembly of that State, and to ask that you will vindicate your
authority, and prove to the people of Georgia, of the South,
and of the country, that you will require Republicans, as
well as Democrats, to obey your laws.

My friend, Mr. Caldwell, has alluded to the reasons that
prompted you to pass the Georgia bill.

The reconstruction acts were violated by the General Assembly of Georgia.   Legally elected members of the legislature were excluded from seats in that body, and men not
entitled to seats were admitted and allowed to participate in
its proceedings.   Mr. Caldwell and myself were the only
white members of the House of Representatives who made
speeches in opposition to the expulsion of the colored members ; we voted against their expulsion ; we protested against
the action of the house in expelling them ; we appealed to
Congress to reseat them ; but we were opposed to the effort
of Governor Bullock to induce Congress to require the members of the General Assembly to take the test oath, and we,
therefore, opposed the bills of Mr. Sumner, of the Senate,
and Mr. Butler, of the House ; but we favored the bill introduced into the Senate by Mr. Edmunds and the bill of Mr.
Carpenter.   In other words, we desired that the colored

members of our General Assembly should be reseated, and that those members who were ineligible under the fourteenth amendment should be expelled, but we were opposed to any further Congressional action.

In accordance with the provisions of the late act of Congress to promote the reconstruction of the State of Georgia, Governor Bullock issued a proclamation, and summoned all persons elected to the General Assembly of said State, as appears by the proclamation of General Meade, to appear on the 1st day of January, at Atlanta, for the purpose of organizing in conformity with the said act of Congress.

Section first of said act is in these words :

"*Be it enacted, &c.*, That the Governor of the State of Georgia be, and he is hereby, authorized and directed forthwith, by proclamation, to summon all persons elected to the General Assembly of said State, as appears by the proclamation of George G. Meade, the General commanding the military district, including the State of Georgia, dated June 25th, 1868, to appear on some day certain, to be named in said proclamation, at Atlanta, in said State ; and thereupon the said General Assembly of said State shall proceed to perfect its organization, in conformity with the Constitution and laws of the United States, according to the provisions of this act."

The "said General Assembly," mentioned in the ninth line of the above section, evidently refers to the persons elected to the General Assembly of Georgia, as appears by the proclamation of General Meade, and the act declares that when they meet, *they* shall proceed to perfect *their own* organization. The exact language is, " and *thereupon* the said General Assembly shall proceed to perfect *its organization* in conformity with the Constitution and laws of the United States, according to the provisions of this act." In violation of that section, Governor Bullock directed one A. L. Harris, the supervisor of the Western and Atlantic railroad, a road belonging to the State of Georgia, to act as clerk or speaker *pro tem.* during the organization of the house of representatives. Mr. Harris is an appointee of Governor Bullock, and can be removed by the Governor at pleasure; he was, therefore, completely under the control of the Governor. By direction of the Governor, Mr. Harris assumed the right to adjourn the house when he pleased. The members were not allowed to participate in the proceedings, except to take the oath required.

Soon after the General Assembly met, on the 10th day of January, by direction of Mr. Supervisor Harris, an attempt was made to read an opinion of the attorney general of Georgia in regard to the eligibility of members under the Georgia bill. Many members believed that the opinion had been prepared by direction of Governor Bullock for the purpose of hindering and interrupting persons duly elected from taking the oath prescribed by the act of Congress. The attorney general is not regarded by the legal profession of Georgia as a lawyer of great ability, and it is well known that he has been a strong partisan of the Governor. He enumerated a large number of officers whom he declared ineligible under the said act. His opinion was endorsed by the General commanding the district of Georgia, General A. H. Terry, an able soldier, and I believe a pure-minded and conscientious gentleman; but the ablest lawyers in Georgia, among whom were Chief Justice Brown and Associate Justice Warner, held that the opinion was erroneous. The opinion was published in the Atlanta papers the day before the General Assembly met, and a copy of one of the papers containing the opinion was placed on the desk of every member. It was also published as a circular, and a copy was sent in an envelope to each member. It was currently reported that the Governor would prosecute for perjury any person who took the prescribed oaths who were in the opinion of the attorney general ineligible, although they might be deemed eligible by the ablest lawyers in the State; and it was announced in the daily papers of Atlanta that able counsel had been retained to prosecute these men. The friends of Governor Bullock prepared a list of persons whom they declared ineligible, and threatened to prosecute any person whose name was on the list who should qualify, by taking the prescribed oaths. A colored member was selected to present a protest against any person taking the prescribed oaths, whose name was on the list. The members were required by Governor Bullock to take the oaths publicly, although many of them had previously qualified and filed these oaths in the office of the secretary of State, as required by law. I have been unable to find in the act of Congress any authority for this interference on the part of the Governor. As members, whose names were on this list, came forward to the clerk's desk and took the oaths prescribed by Congress, the colored member who had been selected for that purpose presented a protest, which was read. These protests were printed, having been carefully prepared beforehand. I do not believe that an intelligent member of the house doubted but that the reading of the opinion of the attorney general, endorsed as it was by the military commander, the presentation and reading of the protests, and the threat to prosecute for perjury, were intended to hinder or interrupt members from taking the prescribed oaths. I know that men, who conscientiously believed that they could take the oaths, were deterred from doing so. They were unwilling to pay the expense of a trial for perjury, and endure the mental excitement that they would suffer during the trial. It is impossible for me to convey to your minds a correct idea of the means resorted to by Gov. Bullock and his friends on that day to prevent men, who were opposed to their schemes, from taking the prescribed oaths. Presiding over, and directing the whole affair, was Foster Blodgett, the evil genius of Georgia at present, the superintendent of the Western and Atlantic railroad, by appointment of Gov. Bullock. As the attempt was being made to prevent men from committing perjury (?) by the reading of the opinion of the attorney general, the reading of the protests, and by other means, which it was necessary to see to understand, and which it is imposible for me to describe, he sat near Mr. Supervisor Harris,

a man who held office under him on the State road, directing the whole affiair. At that moment Mr. Blodgett was
himself under indictment for perjury in the United States
court for having falsely taken the "iron-clad" oath to get
an office, and perhaps (?) for that reason he was anxious
that other men should not be similarly situated.

I was indignant at this open and wilful violation of the
law of Congress, and I objected to the course adopted to
intimidate members. I felt that the Republican party and
Congress were being used to further the ends of corrupt men.
I love the cause advocated by the Republican party as I do
my life. I perilled my life on the battle-field to save my
country, and love the party that conducted the Government
during the dark days of rebellion almost as I do the flag of my
country. Do you wonder, then, that I was indignant when
I saw that party being used by wicked men, as I thought,
to gratify their ambition and plunder my adopted State?
Do you wonder that I, a Northern man and a Union soldier,
was indignant when I saw my party thus disgraced in the
eyes of Southern men, some of whom had fought in the Confederate army, when the whole scheme was directed by a
man then under indictment for perjury—a man who had
fought in the rebel army, and who had assisted to organize
a vigilance committee to *murder Union men?*

Mr. Harris would not recognize my right to speak, although I was a duly elected member of the house and he was
not, and had no legal right to be where he was. I dis-
puted his right to dictate to me, a representative of the
people, and he ordered two fellows to arrest me, whom he
called sergeants-at-arms. I refused to be arrested by them,
and one of them drew a pistol to shoot me. There was a
scene of confusion which I will not attempt to describe. It
is said that I was excited. I presume I was, if the indigna-
tion I felt manifested itself in my appearance. It was evi-
dent that a majority of the members were opposed to the
course pursued by Blodgett, Harris, and their allies, and we
appealed to General Terry. He pronounced their proceed-

ings outrageous, and prevented the further reading of the protests. The enormity of the offence will be apparent to you when you remember that we were duly elected representatives of the people, summoned in conformity with a law of Congress to meet and organize the house to which we belonged, and that a man acting without authority of law assumed to dictate to us what we should say, and because we refused to recognize his authority appointed men to arrest us— men who had no more right to do so than the man who appointed them. Do you ask why we permitted this man thus to violate your law? I answer, that General Terry endorsed the action of Governor Bullock, and thus behind this man Harris stood the military power of this Republic. Suppose that President Johnson, a few months ago, when he wished to control the action of Congress, had been able to overpower the majority by military force, what would have been the result? What would have become of our liberties? General Terry put a stop to some of the arbitrary acts of Harris, but our organization was delayed, and Harris refused to allow the house to perfect its organization in conformity with law, according to the provision of the act of Congress. The organization of the house would have been perfected in two days but for the illegal interference of Governor Bullock. It was, however, eighteen days before it was organized. During that time there was not a day passed but that the act of Congress was openly, wilfully violated.

Section 4 of said act is in these words :

"*And be it further enacted*, That the persons elected, as aforesaid, are entitled to compose such legislature, and who shall comply with the provisions of this act by taking one of the oaths or affirmations above prescribed, shall thereupon proceed in such senate and house of representatives to which they have been elected respectively to reorganize said senate and house of representatives respectively by the election and qualification of the proper officers of each house."

If I understand the above section, all persons elected to the General Assembly, as appears by the proclamation of

General Meade, who complied with the provisions of the act by taking the prescribed oaths, were entitled to participate in the reorganization of the General Assembly.

It will be noticed that section 1 of said act provides that the persons elected, as appears by the proclamation of General Meade, shall *organize*, in order that the prescribed oaths may be taken. Section 4 provides that " the persons elected as aforesaid who shall comply with the provisions of the act by taking one of the oaths prescribed by said act shall *reorganize*." It appears clear to my mind that the intention of Congress was to allow the persons named in the said proclamation of General Meade to *organize* by the election of temporary officers for the purpose of " swearing in " the members, and that those persons named in said proclamation who should take the prescribed oaths should proceed to *reorganize* by the election of permanent officers. If this is not the meaning, I must confess that I do not understand its meaning. If that was the intention of Congress, you must admit that the action of Governor Bullock, of Mr. Harris, and of General Terry, who sustained them, was unauthorized by law. In other words, that they violated the law and usurped authority.

General Terry organized a military commission to inquire into the eligibility of members of said General Assembly who, in conformity with law, had taken the prescribed oaths ; and he ordered men not to participate in the proceedings of the senate and house of representatives, to which they had been elected respectively, who had qualified according to law. He decided that three members of the house and two members of the Senate who had duly qualified should not participate in the organization. I have examined the act of Congress in vain to find the authority to organize a military commission for such a purpose.

Before the General Assembly was organized, persons were allowed to take the seats of some of the members who failed to qualify, upon the ground that they had the next highest number of votes. That was done in violation of the law of

Congress, and in violation of the law of Georgia, as Mr. Caldwell has shown you. Thus has your authority been defied ; thus has the law been overridden, and thus has the General Assembly of Georgia been illegally organized.

We appear before you to ask that you will vindicate your authority ; that you will not allow any person to violate your laws, no matter what may be his position. General Terry is a man for whom I have a high regard—I may almost say affection—but if he were my brother, I would not approve of his acts. If an officer of the army may, with impunity, violate one of your laws, what law may not military officers violate, and what will become of our Republic? I am unable to account for the course pursued by General Terry, unless he was first led by cunning men to take a position which was not a violation of law, but that he was led on, step by step, until he did violate the law. I believe that General Terry has been governed by honest motives, and that in the name of loyalty he has been induced to do what, in my opinion, he would not do again under similar circumstances. General Terry is a distinguished officer of the Republic. No man admires his course during the war more than I do ; but I cannot believe that Congress will sustain even so distinguished an officer when he violates the law.

A committee of Republican citizens of Georgia, several of whom are members of the General Assembly of that State, have come to Washington for the purpose of informing Congress that the act to promote reconstruction in that State has been violated, and to ask that the General Assembly may be reorganized in accordance with law. Mr. Caldwell and myself appear before you to-day to represent that committee. It has been stated that we come to Washington a self-constituted committee ; that the great mass of our people, both Republicans and Democrats, are opposed to any further legislation. I pronounce the statement false, no matter from whom it may come. Our people have been shocked by the usurpations of Governor Bullock, and I must confess frankly that very many of them have but little hope that Congress will interfere. The Democratic party *en masse* oppose his policy, and so do the ablest Republicans in Georgia. Such men as Chief Justice Brown, Hon. A. T. Akerman, the United States district attorney, and Hon. Joshua Hill, the great Union leader of Georgia, do not sustain him. There are two Republican organizations in Georgia. We represent one of those organizations—"The National Republican Club of Georgia"—which numbers among its members many of the ablest Republicans in that State. We have been sent here by that club. We are Republicans, and not Democrats; and as Republicans we expose the usurpations of a Republican governor, whom we all supported, and whom some of us did much to elect. We do this with regret, but we do it from a sense of duty to our State and to our party.

I am chairman of a committee which represents a majority of the legally elected members of the General Assembly, and I know that I represent them when I say to you that our General Assembly has been illegally organized, and that we desire that it shall be reorganized in accordance with law.

It is natural that you should ask us what good will be accomplished by a reorganization of our General Assembly. I will state briefly some of the means used by Governor Bullock and his ring to get control of that body, and what I believe to be the reasons that have induced him to labor with such desperation to secure the control of our legislature. The colored members of the General Assembly of Georgia were expelled in September, 1868. An appeal was made to Congress, signed by a large number of the Republican members of that body, praying that Congress would undo the wrong that had been done, and reseat the expelled members. Mr. Caldwell and myself united with the other Republican members in making that appeal. It was presented to Congress in December by Governor Bullock. He also presented a memorial to Congress upon the same subject, in which he advanced the idea that the legislature had not been legally organized, because the members were not required to take the "test oath," and that on that account the State had not been reconstructed. The entire Republican party of Georgia had recognized the fact that the State was reconstructed. Governor Bullock had taken that position also. He had been inaugurated as *Governor;* the military authority had been withdrawn ; United States Senators had been elected, and the Governor had given them certificates of election ; the State had cast its vote for electors of President and Vice President ; the Republican party, as well as the Democratic party, had nominated and voted for Republican candidates for electors of President and Vice President; the Governor had performed the duties required of him by the constitution as Governor of the State, by issuing commissions to officers, approving bills passed by the legislature, signing warrants, drawing money from the treasury, &c. The theory of the Governor was startling to the thinking people of Georgia, both Republicans and Democrats. The ablest Republicans in the State opposed his policy. Mr. Sumner introduced a bill into the Senate to carry out the views of the Governor, and the fight commenced. It has been kept up from that time until now. We hoped and expected that it had ceased when the Carpenter bill was passed by Congress. The theory of Bullock had not been sustained by that body, but he appeared to yield in good faith. Soon after the legislature met we became satisfied that it was his intention to control the legislature by fraud and violence, if it could be done in no other way. He resorted to the means that I have already mentioned to accomplish that result. Through all this controversy, from December, 1868, until now, he has manifested a willingness to take any position that was necessary for him to accomplish the great object—to get control of the legislature. He performed all the duties of a governor, and claimed to be Governor until it was necessary to take the position that the State had not been reconstructed, that he might urge Congress to require the members of the General Assembly to take the " test oath " in the reorganization of that body.

That he might secure the passage of a bill to reorganize the General Assembly, he told you that the seating of men in the place of the expelled colored members was an outrage, because they did not have a majority of the votes cast; but, to secure the control of the legislature, he now advocates the seating of men in the place of ineligible members who did not have a majority of the votes cast. Can you sustain such a man? He has spent months of incessant labor to accomplish his object. He has spent thousands of dollars. He has given costly dinners to Senators and members of Congress, that he might have a favorable opportunity to influence them in his behalf. Where did the money come from to pay all these expenses? The people of Georgia would like to know. Why all this extravagance? It has been done in the name of loyalty, for the protection of the loyal people of Georgia and for the colored men, but I believe that he has been actuated by other motives—

First. To elect Foster Blodgett to the United States Senate.

Second. To sell to the State of Georgia the building now occupied as the Capitol, and known as Kimball's Opera House.

Third. To cover up financial operations.

Fourth. To carry out certain railroad schemes.

Fifth. To get rid of the treasurer, that he may run his arms into the State treasury.

To elect Foster Blodgett and get rid of Dr. Angier, the treasurer, it is not only necessary that he shall control the General Assembly, but it is also necessary that he shall take the position that all the legislation of the past two years has been illegal. Georgia is a great State. It is truly the empire State of the South; and it is simply monstrous to propose to *rip up* all this legislation to accomplish such a sult. He has illegally drawn from the bank in New York, where the State bonds are deposited, more than fifty thousand dollars—money belonging to the State of Georgia; and to cover up this transaction it is, we believe, the intention of the Governor and his friends to sell to the State for a capitol an unsuitable building at an exorbitant price. I am informed that never in the history of Georgia has money been spent by a governor so lavishly as by Governor Bullock; nevertheless the treasurer has saved thousands of dollars to the State by refusing to pay warrants signed by the Governor. The treasurer is, therefore, a dangerous man, and he must be put out of the way.

I am aware, gentlemen, that I have made grave charges against Governor Bullock, but I believe that I can sustain them by proof, if you desire it. These, gentlemen, in my opinion, are some of the reasons that have actuated Governor Bullock to make such desperate efforts to get control of our General Assembly. To accomplish these results he has passed sleepless nights, and has spent thousands of dollars, and at last was obliged to violate your law that he might succeed. If we can be allowed to organize our legislature in accordance with the letter and spirit of the law of Congress, Governor Bullock cannot control it, and we can save our State from being plundered. We shall have a Republican majority in both houses; we will ratify the fifteenth amendment, and pass laws to protect our people.

I appeal to you, gentlemen, to listen to our prayer, I appeal to you to assist us to save our State from ruin.

Messrs. Foster Blodgett, E. Tweedy, Benjamin Conley, and Judges Harral, J. R. Parrott and Wm. Gibson, of Georgia, have come to Washington in the interest of Governor Bullock. Messrs. N. L. Angier, J. H. Caldwell, J. Bowles, C. K. Osgood, A. J. Williams and myself have come to oppose the schemes of Governor Bullock and represent the people of Georgia. We all claim to be Republicans.

During the war, Governor Bullock had charge of one division of the Southern Express Company, and in various ways assisted the rebels. I have already alluded to the record of Mr. Blodgett. Mr. Tweedy was an officer in the rebel army; so was Judge Parrott. I have never heard anything of the record of Judge Harral. Judge Gibson was a rampant rebel. He was colonel of a regiment in the confederate army, and since the war was elected judge, on account of his war record, over a Union man who was supported by

Union men. Mr. Conley was a Union man, and I believe him to be a good man ; I regret that he is in bad company. Messrs. Bullock, Blodgett, Tweedy and Conley live in Augusta, and belong to a ring that now control the Republican party in the interest of Blodgett and Bullock. Gibson, Parrott and Harral are judges of the superior courts, and must obey the commands of their masters, or lose their positions if Bullock is successful. None of these men except Judge Parrott did much to aid in the work of reconstruction, except as members of the Constitutional Convention. Judge Gibson opposed the Congressional plan of reconstruction until the very day that Governor Bullock was elected, when he was suddenly converted. Paul was suddenly converted, but his was not a political conversion. Dr. Angier was a citizen of Georgia when the war begun. His office was the headquarters of the Union men of Atlanta, and when he found that the State would secede he left the State with his family. He has been a Republican since that time. Mr. Caldwell was a minister during the war and took no part in the rebellion. Colonel Bowles was an officer in the Union army. Mr. Osgood and Mr. Williams were Union men, and had nothing to do with the rebellion. As I have before stated, I was an officer in the Union army during the war, and I have been a Republican from my boyhood. In short, our committee is composed of Union men, none of whom held office in the rebel army or aided the rebellion, and all have acted with the Republican party of Georgia since its organization. Some of our delegation did much to build up the Republican party in Georgia, and have labored hard on the stump and in the committee room to promote the cause of reconstruction ; but nearly all of the Bullock delegation were officers in the rebel army. Nevertheless, there are men who would make you believe that we are rebels and Democrats, while the Bullock committee are simon pure Union men and Republicans.

Those with whom I act do not appeal to you as partisans. We appeal to you as Georgians.

We do not ask you to legislate for the Republican party, but we do ask that you will not legislate the Republican party of Georgia out of existence. We feel that we have a right to ask that.

You passed the act to promote the reconstruction of Georgia because legally elected members had been illegally expelled, and men who were not elected were voted into their seats. That was done by Democrats to get control of the General Assembly. Precisely the same thing has been done by Bullock and his friends, who claim to be Republicans. They have done it for the same reason the Democrats did— to get control of the General Assembly. When the Democrats did wrong you reorganized our General Assembly. I am convinced that you will compel Republicans to obey the laws as well as Democrats. If you do not, I assure you that the people of Georgia will overwhelmingly defeat the Republican party at the next election. Up to this time Bullock and his friends are responsible for their illegal proceedings, and not the Republican party of Georgia, for enough Republicans have opposed his schemes to prevent the party from being responsible for his acts; but if Congress and the national Administration sustain the usurpation of Bullock, the Republican party of the nation becomes responsible for his acts. His policy becomes the policy of the national Republican party. I ask you, gentlemen, can the party carry such a load? If you seat Foster Blodgett in the chair of Webster, of Clay, or of Calhoun, will it not be a little bigger load than the party can carry? I think so, gentlemen; and, therefore, as a Republican, I ask that you will not legislate the party out of existence both in Georgia and in the other States of the Union. I have great confidence in New England; she can carry a pretty big load; but I fear that Blodgett and Bullock would be a little too much, even for the land of the Puritans. What would become of New York, Pennsylvania, Ohio, Illinois, and Indiana if an appeal is taken from you to the people, as it will certainly be in a few months, if you sustain the usurpations of these bad men?

I repeat, gentlemen, that I do not ask you to legislate for the Republican party, but you know that we have a wily opponent, ready to take advantage of every mistake we make. I see before me one of the ablest leaders of the party opposed to us. What can we say when these men go before the people and tell them that a military commission decided the question of the eligibility of the members of a legislative body ; that duly elected representatives of the people who had qualified according to law were expelled by a military order ; that Congress permitted this outrage upon American liberty to be perpetrated by sustaining the perpetrators ; that when Democrats put minority candidates in the place of ineligible members, it was considered an outrage ; that when Republicans did the same thing, they were not interfered with ; that when the Republican ox was gored Congress interfered, but when the Democratic ox was gored Congress refused to take notice of the offence ; that to send to the United States Senate a rebel officer who had falsely taken the *"iron-clad"* oath to get an office, and was under indictment for perjury in a United States court, the legislation of two years' standing was *ripped up*; that business transactions involving millions of dollars were cancelled ; that an honest treasurer, a Union man and a Republican, was put out of office that a corrupt ring might thrust their arms into the treasury of the State and plunder an impoverished people?

If we answer that all this has been done in the name of loyalty, will not the people reply, Oh ! loyalty ; what crimes are committed in thy name !

But, gentlemen, you are statesmen ; you know what is best to be done in our case, and I feel assured that you will not sustain these bad men ; I feel assured that you will do right. You have been sustained by the people thus far, and I believe that you will so act that they will sustain you in the future as in the past. We have attempted to state to you, truthfully and frankly, our condition ; we have come several hundred miles to lay these facts before you and to make this appeal ; we have done our duty ; we believe that you will do yours as honestly as we have done ours ; we leave our case in your hands, begging you to remember that a million of people watch with anxiety for your decision.

A Northern man by birth, a Georgian by adoption, a Union soldier, a Republican, I appeal to you to save my State from this "ring" of bold, bad men, who have, by violence and fraud, got control of the legislature of the State.

J. E. BRYANT.

P. S.—I hand you herewith the argument of Hon. Geo. N. Lester, of Georgia, against the "provisional" idea of Gov. Bullock.

J. E. B.

APPENDIX.

The following drafts were drawn by Governor Bullock on the Fourth National Bank, New York, the amounts not reported by him or paid into the State treasury, but used by him without any appropriation, and in direct violation of law :

No.   NEW YORK, *October* 29, 1868.
Fourth National Bank of the city of New York, pay to the order of C. Burk seventeen thousand dollars.
                        RUFUS B. BULLOCK,
                                Governor of Georgia.

No.   NEW YORK, *December* 3, 1868.
Fourth National Bank of the city of New York, pay to the order of R. B. Bullock eight thousand dollars. Charge account of State.
                        RUFUS BULLOCK,
                                Governor of Georgia.

                        December 12, 1868.
Pay to the order of H. F. Kimball ten thousand dollars, and charge same to the account of the State of Georgia.
                        RUFUS B. BULLOCK, *Governor.*
To the Fourth National Bank, New York.

The house adopted a report—86 to 37—in reference to the above illegal proceedings, in which it states : " No emergency existed which demanded of Governor Bullock this extraordinary departure from the law. His Excellency acted in direct violation of the known will of the legislature."

Besides the above $35,000 illegally drawn and used by him without warrant or appropriation, in open defiance of law, after being fully put upon his notice by the General

Assembly by a vote of over two to one, the Governor went directly to New York and drew the following draft:

$20,000.   NEW YORK, *March* 27, 1869.

At sight, pay to the order of H. F. Kimball twenty thousand dollars, value received, and charge the same to the account of the State of Georgia.

RUFUS B. BULLOCK, *Governor.*

To the Fourth National Bank, New York.

None of which has ever found its way into the State treasury, thus assuming arbitrary powers, wilfully overriding both the constitution and the laws.

He has paid attorneys over fifteen thousand dollars, nine thousand of which was paid in less than thirty days, as retainers, hoping to buy influence.

On the 21st of November, 1868, the cashier of the Georgia National Bank presented the Governor's draft on the Fourth National Bank of New York for $25,000, and voluntarily states that it was to cover Governor Bullock's individual indebtedness to this bank.

The General Assembly appropriated as the salary of the attorney general $2,000; the Governor has paid him over $6,000.

He has paid out of the State treasury nearly two thousand dollars to light Kimball's Opera House, when the building had not been used for State purposes over six times at night, none of the State offices being kept open nights.

He has paid under a pretence as guard of Executive Mansion, at Milledgeville, $1,400 a year, when responsible parties in that city propose to take special care of the buildings and grounds solely for the use of the grounds.

In 1868, he paid eight Executive clerks, besides his two secretaries, when the law allowed only the two secretaries.

Last year the legislature restricted him to one clerk, besides his two secretaries; he has drawn his warrants for five, besides his secretaries.

The appropriations for 1868 were only for the latter half of the year 1868. Still, for the public printing of 1869, he, in violation of law, drew ten thousand back on 1868, notwithstanding the house, by a vote of over three to one, directed him to charge it as an advance on the printing fund of 1869. This he did that he might save his $25,000 printing fund to silence the mouths of the press.

By a false construction of the 23d section of the appropriation bill, he has drawn warrants for over one hundred thousand dollars, mostly of the class that have heretofore been drawn on the contingent fund. This is independent of the contingent fund of $20,000, which, all but a few dollars, he exhausted in less than six months, mostly for *incidental* expenses of executive department. He drew warrants for $6,000 for arresting three fugitives, and they all absconded shortly after the warrants were drawn. From $50 to $200 has heretofore been the rewards for fugitives.

As an evidence of his interest in the Kimball Opera House, a portion of which is temporarily used as a State house, he labored to secure the influence of the State treasurer in favor of paying said Kimball $25,000 yearly rent for only a portion of the least valuable part of a building that could not have cost Kimball over $100,000, reserving to himself all the first-story front on the main street, most the entire basement, and a large number of rooms in the upper two stories. The acknowledged purpose of the Bullock ring is to sell this house to the State for $400,000, that could not have cost Kimball over $150,000 with all its fixtures.

The law requires the net earnings of the Western and Atlantic railroad (which road belongs to the State) to be paid into the State treasury monthly. The payment for the month of September is the last that has been received. Governor Bullock is the chief officer of the road. Former administrations paid into the State treasury, of net earnings, from $30,000 to $50,000 monthly. The road is a main trunk road, and said, by the best of judges, to be doing more business now than it ever did before. Captain Jones, who had been State treasurer eight years, in his report of July 1, 1867, puts the net earnings at $50,000 per month through the year. The Macon and Western railroad, which is one of three roads fed from this State trunk, and but little over half as long as the State trunk, pays of net earnings about $30,000 a month. The other two in about the same proportion. Certain amounts are known to have been paid and loaned to individuals, not for any service in behalf of the road, but as is believed to purchase influence and adherents. The recipients are mostly Democrats, or so claim, who sustain Bullock, but abuse President Grant and the Republican members of Congress and their policy.

There are many other illegal transactions which we have not space to mention.

N. L. ANGIER,
Treasurer of Georgia.

WASHINGTON, D. C.. *February* 9, 1870.

Before the Judiciary Committee of the Senate, on Saturday, February 12, 1870, Judge Gibson, in behalf of Governor Bullock, read an argument, to which—

Mr. CALDWELL replied in substance as follows :

Mr. Chairman and Gentlemen of the Judiciary Committee :
Governor Bullock's counsel, Judge Gibson, asserts that there was "no loyal government in Georgia" prior to the passage of the late act of Congress to promote reconstruction in that State. I will, as briefly as possible, answer the general assumption which seems to underlie his statement, viz, that if the present organization of the legislature is set aside as illegal, it will be reorganized in such way as to give up the control of the body to persons who are not "loyal;" that is, to Democrats. I have shown in the statement I made before you on Wednesday last, that the original composition of the General Assembly was decidedly Republican. If that legislature did some bad things, it should be remembered that Republicans helped to do these bad things, and many of those who did so are now acting with the Governor. What guarantee have you, then, that when left to themselves they will not do other things equally bad? There were several strict party votes, among them that which elected the speaker, from which it appeared that there was a Republican majority of one in the house and twelve in the senate. Since then the Republican majority has been increased by the deaths which have occurred.

Had each member been left to his own conscience, in the late organization, to qualify or not, just as the law allowed him to do, still holding him amenable in case of perjury, it is likely that a sufficient number would have refused to qualify to make a Republican majority in the two houses of fifteen or twenty. Some viewed the oath prescribed in the last act as more stringent than any previously required, and no amount of persuasion could have induced them to take it; while others, who felt that they could conscientiously take it, were threatened and intimidated so that they refused to qualify. If those who have been put in as minority candidates were expelled, and others who were deterred from swearing were allowed to resume their places, the body would still not be under the control of those whom the learned judge *now* regards as *disloyal;* that is, of Democrats. I inferred, from conversing privately with two of the learned judges who are engaged in this defence of Governor Bullock's policy, that Congress would not act on this case in a way to take the legislature out of the hands of Republicans and give it into the hands of Democrats. While I have shown that a fair and just enforcement of your law will not give the control of the legislature to the Democrats, I insist that you will not allow the law to be violated simply in order to give the control to the Republicans. We have the assurance from you that "justice and fair dealing" shall be the rule of your action; and any argument which assumes that mere party ascendancy will be the rule, is a tacit impeachment of your integrity as honorable and fair-minded legislators. Supposing, then, that the minority men were excluded from the house of representatives, how would the matter stand in that branch of the legislature? The late election for speaker shows that McWhorter, Governor Bullock's candidate, received 76 votes, and Col. Bryant 54. Five Democrats voted for McWhorter, and five scattered, making ten. Bryant received six Republican and forty-eight Democratic votes. From this there appears to have been, at that time, seventy-two Republicans and fifty-eight Democrats in the house; so it would require the admission of fifteen Democrats to overcome the Republican majority in that branch, and an equal number, I think, would be required in the senate.

The minority candidates were seated after the election of speaker, but before the election of the other officers. No calculations of a permanent Republican majority should be considered in the settlement of this question, which is one of law and justice and good faith. After all, such calculations might prove disastrous. It was Speaker McWhorter's rulings which led to the expulsion of the colored members, and many of the Bullock Republicans "dodged" the question, or voted against them.

Your attention has been directed to the leading idea of the Governor's party, viz: that the purpose of the late act of Congress was to set aside the first organization of the legislature as illegal, and render all its acts void, and especially to invalidate the election of United States Senators and State house officers. This construction of the meaning of the act grounds itself upon the idea that the number of ineligible persons supposed to be in the body vitiated the whole body and all its acts.

Now, if we grant that all were really ineligible that Governor Bullock, Judge Gibson, and the other learned judges* with him claim, I would respectfully ask if their conclusion would be legitimate? The Governor's party claim that twenty-eight have been declared ineligible, though the judgment of the military board was actually pronounced in only five cases—three in the house and two in the senate. The larger number would only be about one-eighth of the whole body of representatives and senators. Can any number less than a quorum of disqualified persons in each house disable the whole body from acting legally? Is not a quorum of properly qualified members competent to act? May not such a body pass any law or do any other act common to legislative assemblies that is not repugnant to the constitution which confers such powers upon a quorum?

Is there any example in the history of legislation, any precedent in parliamentary law, to show that a constitutional quorum is not a competent legislative body? If not, how can the presence of one-eighth of the whole number, being ineligible, invalidate all the proceedings of the body? How

---

*Judges Parrot and Harrall.

many ineligible persons in such a body are necessary to make the body illegal and vitiate all its acts, if less than a quorum can do it? If any number less than a quorum can do it, what shall be said of the present organization, with eight ineligible persons in one branch and two in the other? We have shown that minority candidates were seated, and that in violation of the act of Congress, of the Code of Georgia, and of parliamentary law in general. Some of them are doubly ineligible. I mention the case of James L. Dunning, the postmaster at Atlanta. He was not elected by a majority—his name does not appear in General Meade's proclamation of June 25, 1868—and yet he was seated in the place of Mr. Winn, who was declared ineligible by the military. At the same time that he thus holds a seat in the Georgia senate, he is the regular postmaster at Atlanta, under a commission from the President of the United States. Holding these two positions at the same time, and enjoying the emoluments of both, he violates the constitution of the State, which he has sworn to support.

In reply to the questions generally which you have put to me, I will state that I express the views of nearly the entire delegation when I say that all we desire, all we ask for, is a stable, good government for the State of Georgia. We have only asked for a remedy for existing evils ; a redress of the wrongs of which we have complained. We are willing for Congress to apply the remedy, to point out the mode of redress, and to save our State from calamity which will inevitably befall it if Governor Bullock's policy is carried out. We do not ask for a reorganization of the present legislature unless Congress chooses to relieve us in that way. We care but little for the irregularities of the present organization, and are willing for it to stand if Governor Bullock may not be allowed to carry out his ruinous designs. If you suffer everything that preceded the "Act to promote reconstruction" to be ripped up and official terms to be extended as the Governor proposes, it will throw us into inextricable confusion, and perhaps involve us in financial ruin. If you recognize the validity of the legislature prior to the expulsion of the colored members, let all the acts of the body up to that time stand ; admit the present senators elect, and confine the official terms within the limits prescribed by the ordinance of the convention and the constitution, we are content, though we are confident that some members are excluded who are justly entitled to their seats. I am as anxious for peace, quiet, and good government as is Judge Gibson ; I have labored four years for reconstruction, and during much of that time he was violently opposed to the reconstruction acts of Congress.

If my verbal answers to your questions in relation to the senatorial election are correctly reported, I think in one of them I must have made an erroneous impression. If so, I desire to correct it in this printed statement. In the tabular statement of that vote which is appended to the remarks I made on Wednesday I show that Governor Brown was elected, but I did not mean that all who are declared ineligible are really so. All my arguments have been designed to show that some were unfairly prevented from qualifying, and it only requires two of this latter class who voted for Mr. Hill to elect him. I believe that there are several who voted for him who are not ineligible under the 14th article. In fact, they all took an oath in July, 1868, that they were not disqualified by the 14th article.

In 'referring to *ineligible* members of the legislature, in the appendix, I apply the term to designate those who were *found* ineligible by the military commission, or declined, neglected, or refused to take either of the oaths prescribed by the act under which the legislature was convened by the Governor. I desire not to be understood as assenting to the ineligibility of these members. Three of them, Messrs. George, Hudson, and Penland, members of the House, were clearly of opinion that they were eligible, but were sensitive and preferred not to serve. Like some others, they would not incur the slightest odium to retain their seats.

Mr. George was elected without opposition by a constitu-

.ency numbering three colored voters to one white, on account of his eligibility under the election order of General Meade. Mr. Penland is said never to have held office prior to the war, and was a decided Union man. Mr. Hudson was forced by conscription to take refuge in a petty office, to escape military service. These gentlemen voted for Mr. Hill.

I do not consider that the ineligibility of members of the legislature, if, indeed, any exists, has been legally adjudicated or ascertained. Col. Bryant and myself, as also Chief Justice Brown, were decided friends of Governor Bullock's administration, as long as we could conscientiously defend it. Col. B. and myself voted for the Chief Justice against Mr. Hill, and neither of us supported Mr. Miller. After the election was over, with all the facts fresh in our recollections, we were constrained to agree with the Chief Justice that it was regular and legal, and ought not to be disturbed. Such, too, was the opinion of District Attorney Akerman, for whom we also voted, against Mr. Miller.

But why canvass this vote at all? Did not the credentials of Hill and Miller, which were signed officially by the Governor, certify that they were legally elected? and is not this a stronger evidence of their right to be seated than any that his Excellency has since adduced to prove the contrary?

GOVERNOR BULLOCK'S PERSONAL ATTACK.

It was not my intention, in any of my remarks, to allude to Governor Bullock in disrespectful terms. I undertook to show wherein I believed that he had done wrong; and in doing so, it was necessary to name him repeatedly; but I did so respectfully, and with a proper regard for the high office which he fills. Instead of answering my arguments in a fair and candid way, he endeavors to lessen their force by a personal assault. I allude to the letter of Foster Blodgett in relation to myself, which the Governor has seen fit to publish in his pamphlet. In regard to Mr. Blodgett, I have said nothing, except to mention him as one who was voted for in the election for Senators. That gentleman has attained so unenviable a reputation, notoriety, throughout the country that I did not see fit to allude to him in any other connection than the one stated. His letter to Governor Bullock discloses one of his characteristic traits, and is a specimen of what are commonly called in Georgia "Blodgett Tricks." He professes to be "very much astonished" at my opposing the organization of the legislature, as if my opposition was a new thing, which he had just found out on the day that he wrote the letter. His Excellency seems also to have shared his surprise, else why did he publish the letter? They both knew that from the day the General Assembly met I have not ceased in the most open and public manner to oppose the organization of the legislature on Governor Bullock's plan. They both know that for more than twelve months I have, with other Republicans of my State, in the most public manner, opposed Governor Bullock's line of policy. They both know that I was one of the first to take a firm stand against that policy, and that I was supported in it by such men as Governor Brown, Colonel Akerman, and many of the ablest Republicans in the State ; that I came with a delegation to Washington last March on purpose to labor, and that I did labor to defeat that policy.

My reason for laying these personal matters before the committee is to show the methods by which Governor Bullock and Mr. Blodgett have sought to have the legislature organized in their own interest. The letter refers to a conversation between Mr. Rice, a member of the legislature, and myself, in regard to the United States Senatorship, and uniting the Republican party. I am represented as requesting Mr. Rice to say to Mr. Blodgett that if the party would elect me Senator for the long term, I would "sustain Governor Bullock, and work to unite the Republicans on the same line." I deny that I authorized Mr. Rice, or any one else, to convey such a message from me to Mr. Blodgett. There was a conversation between Mr. Rice and myself, as there was between others and myself, on that subject, but nothing transpired of a nature to commit me to a support of

Governor Bullock's policy. I labored to unite the Republicans until the task became hopeless. My plan of harmony was very different from Governor Bullock's. My plan was to unite on the restoration of colored members, the ratification of the 15th article, and general amnesty—relief from all political disabilities. Governor Bullock's plan, ever since the expulsion of the colored members, was to get Congress to pass a bill, not merely to restore the colored members, but to declare the legislature illegal, in order to procure another senatorial election. All the time believing that Messrs. Hill and Miller were duly elected, I knew the party could not be united on *any* senatorial election. The issue was never a personal one, but one of principle and moral right.

I may mention some other "tricks" of Mr. Blodgett and the Governor to "unite" the party on their plan.

About the same time that the conversation with Mr. Rice occurred, Mr. A. L. Harris, the Governor's clerk *pro tem.*, and railroad supervisor, said to me that I should have any place I wanted in his department if I would yield my opposition to the Governor. About two days before, a minister of the gospel came to me and said that one of the Governor's employees, on the State road, had called on him, and desired him to convey a message from the Governor, Mr. Blodgett, and Colonel Farrow to me, the purport of which was that I should have choice positions for myself and son, and for my two brothers and their sons, if I would fall in line with them. The messenger stated, also, that an interview was desired by all the parties. I declined the interview. A few days after this, my two brothers came to me, and, with tears in their eyes, entreated me to yield for their sakes. I answered them that I would stand or fall upon the right.

By fraud, treachery, violence, and attempts at bribery, the Governor and his friends have labored to secure a legislature which they hoped to make entirely subservient to their wishes. How far they have succeeded by such means I do not pretend to say. There is one rule, however, by which the people of the State will judge. There were thirty-six Republican members of the General Assembly who refused, in 1868, to vote for Foster Blodgett. How many will vote against him in 1870 remains to be seen. Governor Bullock's report of my first argument before the committee is incorrect. He has had several statements altered to serve his own purpose, so as to make me say things which seem to favor his views. The printed copies which we have submitted contain my remarks just as I delivered them, except one or two corrections in regard to the vote for senators. The Governor tries habitually to practise deception among all with whom he has any dealings of a political character, and this peculiarity accounts for his estrangement from some of the most distinguished members of the Republican party in Georgia.

They saw that instead of directing his administration, as a wise ruler should, to gain the confidence and good-will of the people of the State, he aimed steadily at merely selfish ends. The popular discontent in Georgia is, in a great degree, attributable to the belief that Governor Bullock's maladministration of the State government meets the approval of Congress and the Executive. The fact that several of the most talented Republicans of the State condemn his persistent efforts to keep alive agitation, serves to convince the people that they can have no repose while the Governor "has his sway."

This will not be wondered at when one of the Governor's most prominent judicial appointees has declared that "there could be no peace in Georgia until Mr. Blodgett was elected a U. S. Senator."

www.ingramcontent.com/pod-product-compliance
Lightning Source LLC
Chambersburg PA
CBHW021558270326

41931CB00009B/1281